The Little Book of Short Prayers

THE LITTLE BOOK OF
SHORT PRAYERS

Compiled by Philip Law

A LION BOOK

This edition copyright © 1998 Lion Publishing

Published by
Lion Publishing plc
Sandy Lane West, Oxford, England
www.lion-publishing.co.uk
ISBN 0 7459 4062 5

First edition 1998
10 9 8 7 6 5 4 3 2 1 0

Acknowledgments
We would like to thank all those who have given us permission to include material in this book. Every effort has been made to trace and acknowledge copyright holders of all the quotations in this book. We apologize for any errors or omissions that may remain, and would ask those concerned to contact the publishers, who will ensure that full acknowledgment is made in the future.

A catalogue record for this book is available from the British Library

Printed and bound in Great Britain by Caledonian International Book Manufacturing, Glasgow

It is an old custom of the servants of God to have some little prayers ready to hand, and to be frequently darting them up to Heaven during the day.

PHILIP NERI

The Lord bless thee, and keep thee:
The Lord make his face shine upon thee,
and be gracious unto thee:
The Lord lift up his countenance upon thee,
and give thee peace.

NUMBERS 6:24–26

May the road rise to meet you.
May the wind be always at your back.
May the sun shine warm upon your face.
May the rains fall softly upon your fields.
Until we meet again,
May God hold you in the hollow of his hand.

OLD GAELIC BLESSING

Eternal Light, shine into our hearts;
Eternal Goodness, deliver us from evil;
Eternal Power, be thou our support;
Eternal Wisdom, scatter our ignorance;
Eternal Pity, have mercy upon us.

ALCUIN OF YORK

8

Let this day, O Lord,
add some knowledge or
good deed to yesterday.

LANCELOT ANDREWES

Bless our home, Father,

that we cherish the bread before there is none,

discover each other before we leave,

and enjoy each other for what we are,

while we have time.

ANONYMOUS (HAWAIIAN)

O GOD OF MANY NAMES
LOVER OF ALL NATIONS
WE PRAY FOR PEACE
IN OUR HEARTS
IN OUR HOMES
IN OUR NATIONS
IN OUR WORLD.
THE PEACE OF YOUR WILL
THE PEACE OF OUR NEED.

GEORGE APPLETON

Lord, thou knowest how busy I must be this day.
If I forget thee, do not thou forget me.

JACOB ASTLEY

Yea, though I walk through the valley of
the shadow of death, I will fear no evil:
for thou art with me.

PSALM 23:4

Eternal God, the light of the minds that know you, the joy of the hearts that love you and the strength of the wills that serve you; grant us so to know you, that we may truly love you, and so to love you that we may fully serve you, whom to serve is perfect freedom.

St Augustine

Grant us grace, almighty Father,
so to pray as to deserve to be heard.

JANE AUSTEN

Give me such love
for God and men,
as will blot out all
hatred and bitterness.

DIETRICH BONHOEFFER

DEAR GOD, BE GOOD TO ME. THE SEA IS SO WIDE AND MY BOAT IS SO SMALL.

BRETON FISHERMAN'S PRAYER

Teach me your ways, O Lord; make them known to me. Teach me to live according to your truth.

PSALM 25:4

All through this day, O Lord,
let me touch the lives of others for good,
whether through the word I speak,
the prayer I breathe,
or the life I live.

Anonymous

O Lord, I do not pray
for tasks equal to my strength:
I ask for strength equal to my tasks.

PHILLIPS BROOKS

Think through me, thoughts of God,
And let my thoughts be
Lost like the sand-pools on the shore
Of the eternal sea.

AMY CARMICHAEL

I ask you o Lord to send your delight into my heart and your love into my senses, and to let your mercy cover me.

THE BOOK OF CERNE

My Lord,
I thank you for having created me.

Create in me a clean heart, O God;
and renew a right spirit within me.

PSALM 51:10

Slow me down Lord,
ease the pounding of my heart
by the quietening of my mind,
steady my hurried pace with the vision
of the eternal reach of time.
give me, amid the confusion of the day,
the calmness of the everlasting hills.

ORIN L. CRAIN

Keep us, Lord, so awake in the
duties of our calling that we may sleep
in thy peace and wake in thy glory.

JOHN DONNE

Teach me to pray,
pray thou thyself in me.

FRANÇOIS FÉNELON

Today, O Lord, I accept your acceptance of me.
I confess that you are always with me and always for me.
I receive into my spirit your grace, your mercy, your care.
I rest in your love, O Lord. I rest in your love. Amen.

RICHARD J. FOSTER

O LORD, BAPTIZE OUR HEARTS
INTO A SENSE OF THE CONDITIONS
AND NEEDS OF ALL MEN.

GEORGE FOX

My God and my all.

ST FRANCIS OF ASSISI

Lord, thou hast been our dwelling place
in all generations.
Before the mountains were brought forth,
or ever thou hadst formed
the earth and the world,
even from everlasting to everlasting,
thou art God.

PSALM 90:1–2

As the rain hides the stars, as the autumn mist hides the hills, as the clouds veil the blue of the sky, so the dark happenings of my lot hide the shining of thy face from me. Yet, if I may hold thy hand in the darkness, it is enough. Since I know that, though I may stumble in my going, thou dost not fall.

ANONYMOUS

O Lord, may I be directed
what to do and what to leave undone.

ELIZABETH FRY

Lord, in union with your love, unite my work with your great work, and perfect it. As a drop of water is taken up into the activity of the river, so may my labour become part of your work. Thus may those among whom I live and work be drawn into your love.

GERTRUDE THE GREAT

FATHER, I AM SEEKING:
I AM HESITANT AND UNCERTAIN,
BUT WILL YOU, O GOD,
WATCH OVER EACH STEP OF MINE
AND GUIDE ME.

ST AUGUSTINE

Lord, you are the deepest wisdom,
the deepest truth,
the deepest love within me.
Lead me in your way.

RICHARD HARRIES

Thou that hast given so much to me,
Give one thing more – a grateful heart.

GEORGE HERBERT

Lord, I have given up my pride
and turned away from my arrogance…
As a child lies quietly in its mother's arms,
so my heart is quiet within me.

PSALM 131:1, 2

God give me work
Till my life shall end
And life
Till my work is done.

WINIFRED HOLTBY

Teach us, good Lord,
to serve you as you deserve:
to give, and not to count the cost;
to fight, and not to heed the wounds;
to toil, and not to seek for rest;
to labour, and not to ask for any reward,
except that of knowing that we do your holy will.

St Ignatius Loyola

O Lord, renew our spirits and
draw our hearts unto yourself,
that our work may not be
as a burden but a delight.

BENJAMIN JENKS

Lord, thou knowest what I want,
if it be thy will that I have it,
and if it be not thy will,
good Lord, do not be displeased,
for I want nothing which you do not want.

JULIAN OF NORWICH

O Lord, I need your grace so much if I am to start anything good, or go on with it, or bring it to completion. Without grace, I have no power to do anything – but nothing is beyond my powers, if your grace gives strength to me.

THOMAS A KEMPIS

SEARCH ME, O GOD, AND KNOW MY HEART:
TRY ME, AND KNOW MY THOUGHTS:
AND SEE IF THERE BE ANY WICKED WAY IN ME,
AND LEAD ME IN THE WAY EVERLASTING.

PSALM 139:23–24

From the cowardice
that shrinks from new truths,
from the laziness
that is content with half-truth,
from the arrogance
that thinks it knows all truth,
O God of truth, deliver us.

Anonymous

Father in heaven, when the thought of you wakes in our hearts, let it not wake like a frightened bird that flies about in dismay, but like a child waking from its sleep with a heavenly smile.

SØREN KIERKEGAARD

Let us live in such a way
That when we die
Our love will survive
And continue to grow. Amen.

MICHAEL LEUNIG

LORD, GIVE US FAITH
THAT RIGHT MAKES MIGHT.

ABRAHAM LINCOLN

O Love that wilt not let me go,
I rest my weary soul in thee:
I give thee back the life I owe,
that in thine ocean depths its flow
may richer, fuller be.

GEORGE MATHESON

LET ME HAVE TWO THINGS
BEFORE I DIE:
KEEP ME FROM LYING,
AND LET ME BE NEITHER
RICH NOR POOR.

PROVERBS 30:7–8

If this day I should get lost amid the perplexities of life and the rush of many duties, do thou search me out, gracious Lord, and bring me back into the quiet of thy presence.

F.B. MEYER

Lord, make me see thy glory
in every place.

MICHELANGELO

The Lord is my pace-setter, I shall not rush,
He makes me stop and rest for quiet intervals,
He provides me with images of stillness,
which restore my serenity.
He leads me in the ways of efficiency;
through calmness of mind,
And his guidance is peace.

TOKI MIYASHINA (BASED ON PSALM 23)

THE THINGS, GOOD LORD,
WE PRAY FOR,
GIVE US THE GRACE
TO LABOUR FOR.

THOMAS MORE

Lord, thou art the living flame, burning ceaselessly with love for man. Enter into me and inflame me with thy fire so that I might be like thee.

JOHN HENRY NEWMAN

You, Lord, give perfect peace to
those who keep their purpose firm
and put their trust in you.

ISAIAH 26:3

Too late I loved you, beauty so old yet always new! Too late I loved you! And lo, all the while you were within me – and I, an alien to myself, searched for you elsewhere.

ST AUGUSTINE

God grant me the serenity to accept the things I cannot change, the courage to change the things I can, and the wisdom to know the difference.

REINHOLD NIEBUHR (ADAPTED)

O God, the source of the whole world's gladness and the bearer of its pain, may your unconquerable joy rest at the heart of all our trouble and distress.

ANONYMOUS

In thy journeys to and fro
God direct thee;
In thy happiness and pleasure
God bless thee;
In care, anxiety or trouble
God sustain thee;
In peril and in danger
God protect thee.

TIMOTHY OLUFOSOYE

O Lord, help us to be
masters of ourselves
that we may be
the servants of others.

ALEXANDER HENRY PATERSON

LORD, HELP ME NOT TO DESPISE OR
OPPOSE WHAT I DO NOT UNDERSTAND.

WILLIAM PENN

O Lord, how long shall I cry for help,
and you will not listen?

HABAKKUK 1:2

Teach me to feel another's woe;
To hide the fault I see;
That mercy I to others show,
That mercy show to me.

ALEXANDER POPE

Most loving Lord,
give me a childlike love of thee,
which shall cast out all fear.

EDWARD BOUVERIE PUSEY

Lord, help me to say 'yes'.

MICHEL QUOIST

O GOD, THE AUTHOR OF PEACE
AND LOVER OF CONCORD,
GRANT UNTO US TO BE SO FIRMLY
ESTABLISHED IN THE LOVE OF THYSELF,
THAT NO TRIALS WHATSOEVER MAY
BE ABLE TO PART US FROM THEE.

ROMAN BREVIARY

O Lord, forgive what I have been,
sanctify what I am,
and order what I shall be.

Anonymous

Our Father in heaven:
May your holy name be honoured.

Matthew 6:9

O make my heart so still, so still,
When I am deep in prayer,
That I might hear the white mist-wreaths
Losing themselves in air!

UTSONOMYA SAN

God be in my head, and in my understanding;
God be in my eyes, and in my looking;
God be in my mouth, and in my speaking;
God be in my heart, and in my thinking;
God be at my end, and at my departing.

SARUM PRIMER

O LORD, THAT LENDS ME LIFE,
LEND ME A HEART REPLETE
WITH THANKFULNESS.

WILLIAM SHAKESPEARE

Lord give us grace
that we may know
that in the darkness pressing round
it is the mist of sin that hides thy face;
that thou art there
and thou dost know we love thee still.

GILBERT SHAW

Keep us, O Lord,
from pettiness;
let us be large in thought,
in word, in deed.

MARY STEWART

God, have mercy on me,
a sinner!

LUKE 18:13

Abide in me; o'ershadow by thy love
Each half-formed purpose and dark thought of sin;
Quench, ere it rise, each selfish, low desire,
And keep my soul as thine, calm and divine.

Harriet Beecher Stowe

GRANT ME TO RECOGNIZE
IN OTHER MEN, LORD GOD,
THE RADIANCE OF YOUR OWN FACE.

PIERRE TEILHARD DE CHARDIN

My life is an instant,
An hour which passes by;
My life is a moment
Which I have no power to stay.
You know, O God,
That to love you here on earth —
I only have today.

ST THÉRÈSE OF LISIEUX

Thou madest me for thyself,
and my heart is restless until
it find its rest in thee.

ST AUGUSTINE

Come, for I need thy love,
More than the flower the dew or grass the rain;
Come gently as thy holy dove;
And let me in thy sight rejoice to live again.

JONES VERY

O GOD, WHO HAS FOLDED BACK THE
MANTLE OF THE NIGHT TO CLOTHE US
IN THE GOLDEN GLORY OF THE DAY,
CHASE FROM OUR HEARTS ALL GLOOMY
THOUGHTS AND MAKE US GLAD
WITH THE BRIGHTNESS OF HOPE.

ANONYMOUS (ANCIENT COLLECT)

Father, not my will
but your will be done.

LUKE 22:42

Lord, let me not live
to be useless.

John Wesley

Drop thy still dews of quietness
Till all our strivings cease:
Take from our lives the strain and stress,
And let our ordered lives confess
The beauty of thy peace.

JOHN GREENLEAF WHITTIER

Incline us, oh God!, to think humbly of ourselves, to be severe only in the examination of our own conduct, to consider our fellow-creatures with kindness, and to judge of all they say and do with that charity which we would desire from them ourselves.

JANE AUSTEN

Father, hear the prayer we offer,
Not for ease that prayer shall be,
But for strength that we may ever
Live our lives courageously.

LOVE MARIA WILLIS

In me there is darkness, but with thee there is light.
I am lonely, but thou leavest me not;
I am feeble in heart, but thou leavest me not;
I am restless, but with thee there is peace;
In me there is bitterness, but with thee there is patience.
Thy ways are past understanding,
but thou knowest the way for me.

DIETRICH BONHOEFFER

O God, make me quick to listen,
but slow to speak
and slow to become angry.

ADAPTED FROM JAMES 1:19

O Immanence, that knows nor far nor near,
but as the air we breathe is with us here,
our breath of life, O Lord, we worship thee.

AMY CARMICHAEL

LORD, MAKE ME AN INSTRUMENT OF YOUR PEACE.
WHERE THERE IS HATRED, LET ME SOW LOVE.
WHERE THERE IS INJURY, PARDON.
WHERE THERE IS DISCORD, VISION.
WHERE THERE IS DOUBT, FAITH.
WHERE THERE IS DESPAIR, HOPE.
WHERE THERE IS DARKNESS, LIGHT.
WHERE THERE IS SADNESS, JOY.

ATTRIBUTED TO ST FRANCIS OF ASSISI

To thee, O God, we turn for peace...
but grant us too the blessed assurance
that nothing shall deprive us of that peace,
neither ourselves, nor our foolish, earthly
desires, nor my wild longings, nor the
anxious cravings of my heart.

Søren Kierkegaard

O LORD, SUPPORT US ALL THE DAY LONG OF
THIS TROUBLOUS LIFE, UNTIL THE SHADOWS
LENGTHEN, AND THE EVENING COMES, AND THE
BUSY WORLD IS HUSHED, AND THE FEVER OF
LIFE IS OVER, AND OUR WORK IS DONE. THEN IN
THY MERCY GRANT US A SAFE LODGING, AND A
HOLY REST, AND PEACE AT THE LAST FOR EVER.

JOHN HENRY NEWMAN

Lord, make me like crystal
that your light may shine through me.

KATHERINE MANSFIELD

O LORD, HELP US TO
REMEMBER THAT BEYOND
OUR BRIEF DAY IS THE
ETERNITY OF YOUR LOVE.

REINHOLD NIEBUHR

Grant Lord, that I may not
for one moment admit
willingly into my soul any
thought contrary to thy love.

EDWARD BOUVERIE PUSEY

May the God who gives us peace make you holy in every way and keep your whole being – spirit, soul and body – free from every fault.

1 Thessalonians 5:23